WELCOME TO THE WONDERFUL WORLD
OF TYPE

Stop and take a look around. Whether you are soaking in the bathtub, picnicking on the patio or waiting for a bus, look around. What kind of type do you see? If you're taking a bubble bath, notice the appealing typeface on the bottle of bubbles. Maybe the handwriting on the love note left on your plate makes your heart flutter. Or if you're waiting at a bus stop, cool typesetting might have caught your eye on the ad by the bench. Amazing typography is everywhere! And now – more than ever – it's becoming a major design element on every project possible: scrapbook pages, cards, journals and home décor pieces.

In *Designing With Type*, these celebrated and ultra-talented designers employ every typographic technique imaginable on their handmade creations. This impressive portfolio reveals the full potential of texture, dimension and style that type has to offer the paper-arts industry. Max out your creative energy as you discover ideas that will spice up your projects with meaningful typography.

Tina is **Myriad**: classic, stylish, yet simple and versatile.

Jennifer is DisProporz: straight-laced, classic, with a bit of playfulness.

Renee is *La Portentia de la Boca*: traditional, dramatic and a little loud.

Nia is **fLip fLOp**: bold and stylish with a bit of sass.

FEATURING THE ARTISTS OF
AUTUMN ❧ LEAVES

Jen is **Kabel**: straightforward with a few well-placed quirks.

Emily is *her own handwriting*: fun, playful and stands out in a crowd.

Ashley is **Corisande**: quiet and very practical, but also tons of fun.

Lisa is **Serifa**: straight, lined up and just a little bit square.

Cathy is **One Forty Seven**: handmade with a bit of homespun chic.

Leslie is **Candice** : fun-loving, lively and just plain groovy.

Marilyn is **Noisebaby**: artsy, silly and not always what you expect.

Jackie is **Suburban**: casual, whimsical and somewhat quirky.

Rhonna is *Porcelain*: sassy, swirly and oh so charming.

Carmen is **Univers**: simple, timeless and always trendy.

Kelli is **Indecision**: creative, messy and likes attention... but dreadfully shy.

Danielle is *Gasoline Alley*: funky and eclectic with a graphic foundation.

{ table of contents

1

CHAPTER ONE

Exploring
typefaces

Have you ever spent more time deciding what font to use on a project than it took to actually make the project? We all have! Any more, thousands of typefaces are available either for purchase or for free. With all these fonts it can be overwhelming to know which one to use. In chapter one, our talented type experts prove how fonts can enhance a layout, complement the meaning of a word or simply add interest to a project. Glance at Jennifer's *My Nerd* layout and see how the technical-looking font correlates perfectly with the subject matter of the page. No matter the topic, you're sure to find type to match. Now start downloading!

A font is a complete set of characters in a style of type. It can be used when referring to metal type or a computer file. A typeface is a style of type, like Times New Roman Bold. A font can contain several typefaces.

Exploring Simba
by Marilyn

Make each word its own text box. Alter the font sizes and color. Use the *Rotate* and *Move* tools to rotate, align and overlap elements. To create the subtitle on the second page, create a text box with a solid fill. Set text to white or clear. Type journaling in two columns. Embellish page with pre-printed transparency and text printed on a clear transparency.

The Biggest and the Smallest
by Lisa

Scan a page from a vintage arithmetic textbook. Add title and print on oatmeal cardstock. Cut out and use on background. Print title in an outlined font on white cardstock; stamp word over letters. Tear small bits of papers and collage everywhere but the letters. Randomly brush white gesso onto page for journaling background.

oppostion

member of the

begin love shut you first COLD last low Happy cold open end little me sad high under quiet big

Under the guise of learning, there is a frequent activity that you request to play. Opposite naming. Most other structured educational pursuits, you tend to scoff at within minutes. Perhaps they aren't challenging or exciting enough to hold your attention. The recitation of the alphabet, the spell your name game, the identification of sounds, counting past ten. But the moment there is any mention of opposites, you are all over it. I name one, you name the other. I attempt to trick you, yet you are fairly savvy at four. I hear the occasional "not (adjective in question)" or "There is no opposite for that one Mommy!" We go back and forth until the list is exhausted. Or until I am.

A widow is a word or part of a word that takes up an entire line at the end of a paragraph.

An orphan is the last word of the previous paragraph that appears at the top of a column. Both of these are visually unappealing. Simple text editing will allow you to fit them into the previous line or column.

i'm so proud

TO: Audrey FROM: Mum

thanks tons

Serif Fonts

Member of the Opposition
by Tina

Use all serif fonts for layout. Make each word a separate text box. Type the word, fill the box with color and change the font color to white. Punch each word into a circle. Adhere to background in different directions. Fill empty spaces with buttons.

Serif Fonts

Scribbles
by Jennifer

Print serif text in outline on heavy cardstock. Cut out with an X-Acto knife and use as a template to scribble colored pencil chalk. Embellish letters with brads or mini rhinestones.

On the Move
by Jen

Use photo-editing software to create a brush from the text *"on the move"*. Create a text box with brown fill. Use the brush to "stamp" the text box in different colors. Add a new layer to the text box. Select the same shade of brown as the text box and type a *"G"*. Select the *"G"* and go to *Edit > Stroke* to create an outline, choosing orange as the color. Use the eraser tool to erase the interior of the *"G"* so the brush work shows. Position the outlined *"G"* in the text box. Print, then hand cut a random zigzag pattern in the text box. Mount on white cardstock. Affix to layout along with two patterned paper strips and a journaling strip.

Introducing Howie
by Nia

Using Photoshop or other editing software, open a photo and set page size accordingly, placing photo in bottom left corner. Use different sans serif fonts to create a font "collage", making sure to incorporate several different font sizes, colors and directions. When printed, add embellishments in the open spaces.

Autumn »→
by Leslie

Print title on the back of cardstock in reverse print. Hand cut with an X-Acto knife. Temporarily adhere to a piece of paper, then run through a corrugator. To make the layout, adhere slices and curves of patterned papers to layout; stitch in place. Add photos, titles and buttons.

It has always been my very favorite of all the seasons. The smells, the sights and the sounds... they all add up to the most beautiful and invigorating time of the year. The colors of red, orange, yellow & green are so inspiring to me. Pumpkins to carve, apples falling from the tree in the backyard. There are so many textures to the landscape - pure 'eye candy'. It's a time for family, homemade baking, and walks in the woods. Every season holds its own beauty, but for me Autumn is THE season that dazzles. I'm so thankful to enjoy it year after year.

SEP OCT NOV

AUTUMN

Notice how Leslie overlaps letters in her title. She tightens up the kerning of a word without going near a computer.

Script Fonts

Love
by Rhonna

Use brushes to create elements and patterned paper. Apply a photo edge around the photo. Use various colors of brushes to add flourishes over and under the photo. Use a Wacom Tablet to write the journaling and title. With the paint bucket tool, color in parts of the title letters for added interest.

Script Fonts

New Clothes
by Marilyn

Cut haphazard arches from various patterned papers. Add journaling before cutting. Hand cut computer-generated words, adhere to page along with photos.

Kite
by Leslie

Make a large text box with an olive fill. Type script title in light gray. Print onto white cardstock. Poke holes all over the word for added dimension. For the journaling, create a cream-colored text box with blue script lettering. Print, then journal over the top.

Mothers
by Jennifer

Trim photos to various sizes. Create journaling in a text box the same size as the photo but trim twice as wide. Fold journaling and add photo to front so the journaling is hidden. Adhere to pages and use photo turns to keep closed. For title, print title outline as WordArt (in Microsoft Word) on scrap paper. Lay over background and poke holes around the word. Add pieces of paper and fabric between the holes and then stitch around the outside.

"Hey Mommy, look at these skid marks I can make! Check it out!" At first, to be honest, I wanted to tell you to stop. I wanted to say, "HEY, you are marking up the driveway." Then I thought....it IS just the driveway. I mean... we drive on it. Sure. Skidmark away,

Skidmarks

dude.

You were so proud.

Peddle, peddle...skid.

Peddle, peddle...skijiiiiiiid.

Alexander   age 6.5   Summer of 2005.

 The journaling font Kelli chose is a perfect balance of mood and legibility. It's grungy enough to match her headline without sacrificing readability.

←# Skidmarks
by Kelli

Using various distressed fonts, print each letter in a decreasing size. Cut out each letter, ink the edges and adhere to layout with foam tape.

The Gap
by Cathy

Print an oversized title and journaling on 8 1/2" x 12" cardstock. Adhere to 12"x12" paper and build layout around it. Hand stitch blue strips and add electrical tape as an embellishment.

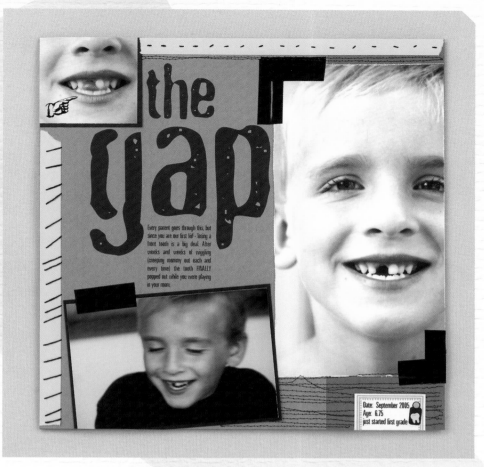

Take inspiration from forms of print, video and web-based media. Take time to notice the combination of fonts, types, as well as the various weights and heights.

Uncomplicated State of Being
by Tina

For the text grouping at the top left, typeset each letter using a block font, arranging the letters to create a mostly solid block. Add additional words around the title block. Distress more with Photoshop brushes. Print title on background paper. Add photos. Stamp on masking tape and add to background, overlapping onto the photos.

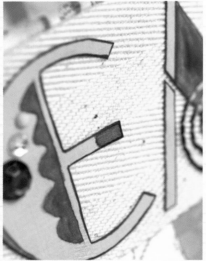

My Nerd
by Jennifer

Create WordArt in Microsoft Word with descriptive words, making sure to choose the circle format. Create additional circles of words. Print and cut into a circle.

Gleam
by Ashley

Cut title from pale blue paper. Using font as a reference, pencil in solid lines, wavy lines and dots. Paint solid-colored portion of font with watercolors, and outline solid lines with black ink. Hand stitch on some of the solid lines. Add rhinestones on the letters.

jams

Modern technology is a wonderous thing. It allows my children to experience so much more in their everyday life. The kids think it's just the grandest thing ever to create their own 'playlists' with their favorite songs. Kaitlyn especially thinks listening to her list is the best. She can jam like nobody's business!
-October 19, 2005

Kaitlyn & the iPod

The iPod
by Renee

Print journaling onto background. Print title on separate page, outlining printed type with glitter. Cut out and stitch to background page in the middle of each letter. Color in rubber-stamped flowers and apply glitter in the centers. Cut a heart from cardstock and stitch to page.

Novelty Fonts

Blooms
by Danielle

Print title onto pink textured cardstock. Embellish with a black pen and fill in with chalk. Cut out the silhouette of the large flowers and journal around the edge.

type
pitfalls

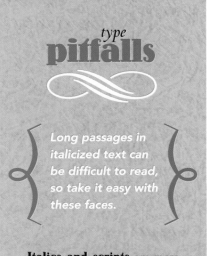

Long passages in italicized text can be difficult to read, so take it easy with these faces.

Italics and scripts are more difficult to read in general because of their tight spacing, their curves and slants and their approximations to handwritten letterforms. Don't ever use them for extended text or no one will read your work. Never use all caps with a script

First Day
by Jackie

For the large flower cutout, print a large flower dingbat (outline only) in very light gray on white cardstock. Adhere photo, then draw the flower petal lines onto the bit of photo they cover. Hand stitch the flower outline and journal around the petals. Trim white cardstock close to the petals' edges and down the left side of photo. To create the center, weave ribbon onto a circle covered with adhesive; trim edges. Embellish with a paper-covered flower brad.

Road Trip
by Renee

Print dingbat and title onto typing paper. Adhere to chipboard strip. Bend and fold entire piece and add a bit of brown ink with a dusting brush. Sand edges; add buttons to accent dingbat. Mat photo on cardstock, then on fabric. Machine stitch title piece over the top.

Here is what you have taught ME.

you, little missy, have your own sense of style already.
You (unlike me) love hot pink and animal prints, sequin encrusted
butterfly and kitty shirts, and I flat out just need to
learn to deal with it.

your
self esteem
is far more important than my love of plain, solid colored neutral clothes.
I'm sorry that it took me awhile to realize that a 5 year old
needs to feel good about themself just as much as a 35 year old does

Install a font-organizing software on your computer that will allow you to sort and arrange your fonts by style and identify favorites. An organizational system will save both time and enhance creativity.

Dingbats

What You Have Taught Me
by Cathy

Print several flower dingbats in different colors, sizes and styles onto cardstock, tags and metal-rimmed tags. Add rhinestones for a finishing touch.

Need some shiny new fonts for your layouts? Go check out a few of our favorites! We're warning you, though – once you get started, it can be hard to stop!

Two Peas in a Bucket *www.twopeasinabucket.com*
Loads of inexpensive, cute fonts that evolve with the scrapbook trends.

Larabie Fonts *www.larabiefonts.com/*
Chose one of 384 free fonts – or spend all night and download each and every one. Don't want to spend all that time on the Internet? You can order all of them on CD for $11.95.

Astigmatic One Eye Typographical Institute *www.astigmatic.com*
A variety of free and pay fonts, including font collections on CD. The fonts here are primarily grunge, digital, and whimsical display fonts.

Font Diner *www.fontdiner.com*
Fonts with a retro feel are what's on the menu at this diner. Even the pay fonts are reasonable. Sold in sets, you can get 6 fonts for about what a couple of Blue Plate Specials would set you back.

Divide by Zero *http://fonts.tom7.com*
Whimsy abounds in these hand-drawn, slightly imperfect yet incredibly charming fonts and dingbats. Use them as doodles or to make your own embellishments.

2

CHAPTER TWO

Creative typesetting

Typesetting has come a long way since primitive days when text was carved into wooden blocks and used as a printing plate. Happily we don't have to do such arduous work to record journaling for a project. And fortunately, we don't even have to line up each letter, one at a time with a composing stick, remembering to line them up backwards so it can be read when printed. Today we just have to do a little typing, click a few times with the mouse and print. In fact, we have countless options of how we arrange our text. We're not bound to straight lines as evidenced by the text used on Danielle's *Star* page or Lisa's *When Ava Met Nana*, which is made from 20 layered text boxes! Celebrate the fact you don't have to carve wood, and go invent some cool typesetting techniques now.

Type is measured in points (for height) -- 72 points per inch. Width of the character is the set width, and includes the width of the character as well as the space which comes prior to the next character.

Best Buddies
by Jennifer

Print journaling to act as the "I" in the title. Cut out other letters from cardstock and adhere to background.

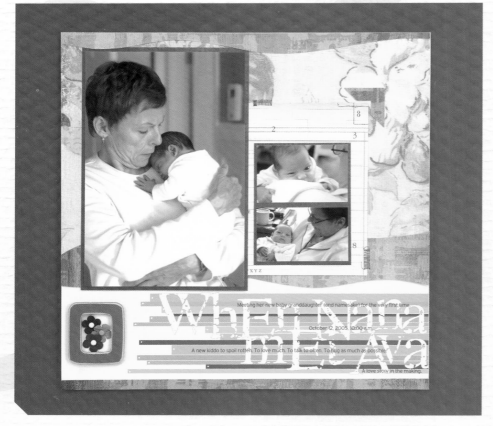

Titles

When Nana Met Ava
by Lisa

In Adobe InDesign create 14 text boxes, pulling the corners and sides to make them into thin strips. Set fill to coordinating colors and insert one bullet in each. Create two additional text boxes for large title words, setting fill to none and text to white/clear with a light gray outline. Use move tools to arrange over colored strips. Create four more text boxes for small word strips, setting fill to none and text to black. Use the move tool to arrange.

Titles

Give and Take →→
by Nia

In Photoshop, create title block in three different color schemes; print all three. With a circle punch, punch out various areas in one of the title blocks. Layer pieces from the other two underneath and on top of circles, making sure the text matches exactly.

happy
we are
together

Family. A little bit of give a little bit of take. 3 generations spending time enjoying each other on a summer afternoon. I love these two with all my heart. Lucky girl indeed.

give & take

o5

Nia used contrast between the modern serif typeface of her title and the bold, clean lines of the sans serif ampersand to make her title really pop.

Words

Star
by Danielle

In Photoshop, layer adjectives to describe the subject. Select a star dingbat, and invert the image so the selected area is inverted. Fill the area with white. Layer that shape on top of the words, thus allowing only the words to show in the star shape and nowhere else. Typeset the title, and print title and star onto green. Print dingbat stars and add to layout with foam tape. Draw black dots around the outside.

Words

I Can Fly
by Tina

Use different sizes of metal, chipboard and plastic letters to create the individual embossed words. Position one letter at a time behind the cardstock, directly on top of the light source (light box or window), and outline the letter with a stylus. Continue in a straight line for each subsequent letter.

Signs
by Tina

Typeset the words as you want them to appear on each of the signs. Reverse print each word individually onto iron-on ink jet paper. Following the directions, iron onto corduroy. Cut into various shapes. Print journaling directly on the background paper, adhere photo and machine stitch signs to background.

Olivia
by Renee

Convert a paw print dingbat into a brush in Photoshop. Create colored squares in Photoshop and add paw print brush in a contrasting color. Insert a text block with text matching the background color. Add text over brushed area until completely covered. Print blocks and machine stitch to page. For the right-hand block, print another square in mirror fashion. Turn over and print text ("*Olivia*") on backside of this block. Cut out small paw prints and adhere to front side of block.

If a flower blooms once, it goes on blooming somewhere forever. It blooms on for whoever has seen it blooming. Sounder. William Armstrong 1969

 Journaling text on a path accentuates the curviness of the hand-drawn type Rhonna used in her title.

Bloom
by Rhonna

Use brushes to create page elements and patterned paper. Use a Wacom Tablet and a calligraphic brush to draw flowers and swirls around photo. Draw title on tablet and use the *Bézier Pen* tool to draw a swirl. Select the *Type* tool, hover the cursor over the path and when it changes, click to type the quote. Stamp text inside flowers for more interest.

Paragraph Treatment

Outbreak
by Marilyn

Add square of white cardstock to burgundy background. For title ("*Outbreak*"), increase the outline thickness of each letter as they progress to the middle of the title and decrease toward the end of the title. Print on cardstock and cut out. For the journaling, increase the thickness of each word as they progress toward the middle of the sentence and decrease toward the end of each sentence.

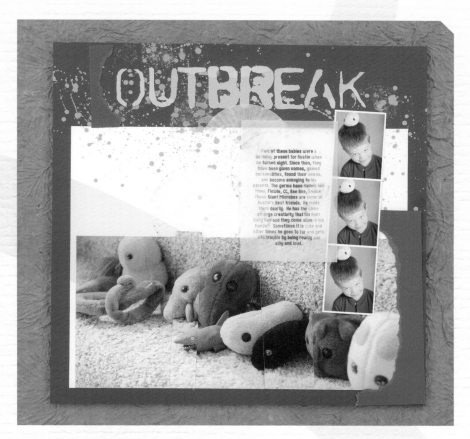

Quote Treatment

Wild and Free
by Leslie

In a word-processing program, create text boxes and arrange into a square graph that is 11" tall. Choose a variety of colors to fill the boxes. Add a centered white letter to the boxes to create a quote. Print on white cardstock and adhere to layout.

type **pitfalls**

If you try to justify narrow columns of text like this one, you'll get gaps.

Don't justify narrow columns of text. Set them aligned on the left and ragged on the right.

27

April Showers
by Danielle

Arrange background text in Photoshop, making the top row large and saturated. As the rows travel down the page, make the type smaller and less saturated. Create flower shapes as negative space within the background text. Print entire image onto aqua cardstock. Subtly outline the flowers with a fine-point marker and use clear buttons as centers. Sand edges of the photos and adhere to layout.

Holiday Cards
by Cathy

Using Adobe Illustrator, type "happy holidays". Convert text to paths and create several different configurations of the phrase (stacked, all in one line, one bigger than the other, etc.). Use the rotate tool to duplicate and rotate the text, starting from the center of the card. Print, then add a snowman or tree made from metal-rimmed tags.

Backgrounds

And a Bicycle
by Kelli

Print each line of journaling onto typing paper. Place labels over the words on the typing paper. Run the paper with labels through the printer again. Remove the labels and affix to layout.

Backgrounds

Why Blog?
by Tina

To create the background, use Photoshop and add layers of text in various opacities, sizes and colors. Print onto background. Add a border of photos around two edges and add a framed photo in the center. Secure a few tissue flowers over the text.

Perpetual Calendar
by Carmen

Typeset the days of the week, months of the year and numbers for the days of the month. Print onto photo paper. Stack the three sections side by side. Fold a piece of chipboard to make an easel so it will stand, and place behind the sections. Bind the pieces to make a perpetual calendar.

Her Natural Beauty
by Emily

Adhere numerous chipboard letters to newspaper, leaving a space in the center for a photo. Sand the chipboard, then apply acrylic paint all over the words and newspaper, leaving some of the newspaper exposed. Attach photo in reserved space. Use embroidery floss, small beads and flower embellishment to create a whimsical photo corner.

Backgrounds

Summer
by Renee

Create layered text in Photoshop that is 8.5"x11". Print onto cardstock. Stitch vellum over some of the text. Add photos, apply rub-ons for accents and title, and stitch on buttons.

"Ideas" Sketch Book
by Jen

Create cover image in photo-editing program; print out and attach to chipboard. Cut cardstock to fit the lower right corner. Spray paint with magnetic paint. Let dry and repeat three or four times. Paint over the magnetic paint with acrylic paint. When dry, attach to the cover and add magnets. Trim shrink plastic to the size of the cover. Attach with binder clips.

Print section dividers on transparencies and trim to 10" long. Trim thick chipboard to make the section dividers. Cover with patterned paper, add quotes and staple on divider. Trim white paper a bit smaller than the chipboard for the journal pages. Punch holes in the dividers and journal pages, and thread onto a file folder clip.

Cut a back cover from chipboard and bind to the front cover with transparency strips. Make a pen holder using ribbon or gaffer tape.

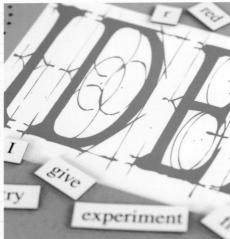

OK. I will admit it. Autumn is the ideal season for photographic opportunity and I embrace it perhaps a bit too enthusiastically. The colors, the outfits, the crisp air, I love it all.

But I think you enjoy it, too. You get to bundle up in your much-loved flannel shirts, overalls and sweaters. And, together, we head to one of our many favorite parks. You get to run around, climb, play and laugh.

And I watch you through my lens, clicking away with the camera to capture that perfect image.

Once and awhile you will stop playing long enough to look at the camera or shoot me a smile. A smile we share for a moment, before you run off again.

Monograms

Sean
by Jennifer

Create a large letter with WordArt in Microsoft Word. Print on cardstock and cut out. Mat letter and stitch around the outside.

NOTE: *There is no background on this layout; it is entirely the 12"x12" "S".*

Monograms

Gift Tags
by Carmen

Design letter on computer; print out. Mat on patterned paper, then again on brown construction paper. Punch hole at the top and thread with ribbon.

Summer Season
by Leslie

In an editing program, crop numerous photos. Number each photo. Change the color, font and opacity of each number so they are all different.

MSF
by Emily

Cover cardstock in different-sized envelopes; adhere with gel medium. Paint with different shades of the same color. Mix hand-drawn and stamped numbers to represent different areas of a person's life.

Five Friends
by Nia

In Word, create a 6"x 6" text box inside which to type title. Set background color to dark red and type words in white, orange, yellow and pink, using appropriate symbols in place of letters. Adhere to corrugated background along with journaling and photos.

Symbols

Symbol Cards
by Tina

Cut shapes from cardstock. Cover with stitched-on buttons. Incorporate on a card front.

3

CHAPTER THREE

Handmade type

Visit almost any preschool class and you'll observe children gluing pasta shells in the shapes of letters. Or you'll see them drawing letters in shaving cream. Nothing is out of the question with preschoolers for how to practice forming letters, and nothing should be out of the question for paper artists. There are no boundaries on what can be used to fashion letters, numbers or words. You'll love Jen's letters made with the Sunday comics and you'll ooh and ahh over Jackie's letters made from her ribbon stash. Pretend you're back in elementary school and see what ingenious media you can use to create text.

White type on a dark background (reverse type) appears smaller than black type on a white background. If using reverse type, select a larger point size and a bolder font.

My Sweet Boys
by Nia

Using Photoshop or other editing software, create number collage (date of photos taken) by placing numbers at various angles, making sure to overlap each number. Once printed on heavy cardstock, choose a patterned paper (or magazine page in this case) and adhere over sheet of printed numbers. Trim around edges. Adhere to left side of layout. Print photo and trim into a large half circle. Print journaling and adhere under large photo.

Austin Versus the Volcano
by Marilyn

Round corners of gray cardstock base. Stamp images as shown. Cut a rounded rectangular shape from orange cardstock. Add a strip of yellow paper across orange cardstock. Write words with orange pencil, in cursive, on yellow cardstock; cut out. Write "*volcano*" with red-orange pencil on red-orange cardstock; cut out. Stitch paperclips to page. Add words inside each paperclip. Journal using rub-ons.

Avoid using typefaces that are very overused, like Helvetica, Arial or Times New Roman. Explore creative alternatives that accomplish the same objective, like Corisande, Univers or Mrs. Eaves.

Hand-cut Letters

Family
by Leslie

Print title in reverse onto cardstock, then cut out with an X-Acto knife. Cut or punch circles and then glue the letters for title onto same color circles to give it a "barely there" look.

Hand-cut Letters

Vital Statistics
by Tina

Create a 12"x12" template of the actual page in Photoshop. Position the text and photos as desired. Print a copy to use as reference for positioning only. Save document. Determine which words will be in which color. Each color will be printed separately. Delete all words that do not need to be printed in that color. Print the mirror image on the back of patterned paper. Do not save document. Re-open original document. Repeat for each type of patterned paper you will be using, until all words have been printed. Hand cut letters and adhere to background paper, using the template as a guide.

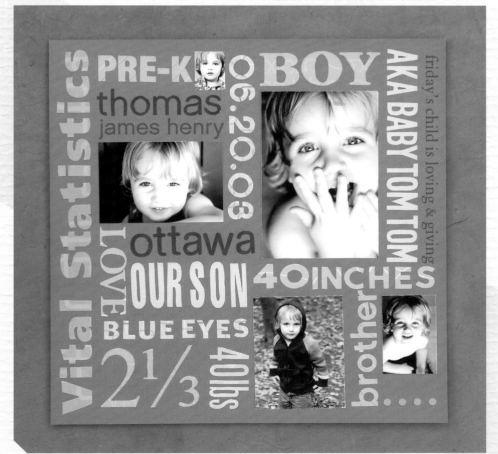

this dad grew WAY too many tomatoes

this mom and dad

celebrated 8 easy years

this kid mastered the tricycle

this kid lost his front tooth

this kid tossed her training wheels

these kids can totally swim

endless summer

endless summer

summer

SUMMER

2005

recap

{ **Using a pre-existing typeface as a template** gives your pages a funky, handmade feeling, without the headache of drawing your own typeface. }

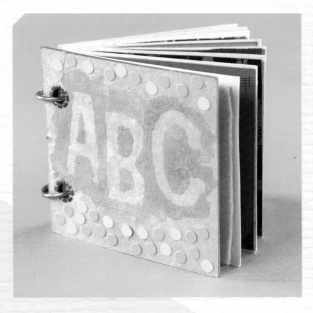

Letterforms Created from Something Else

ABC Book
by Kelli

Make an alphabet book with each letter made from a different creative medium. Staple the letter "*J*" or arrange brads in the shape of an "*M*".

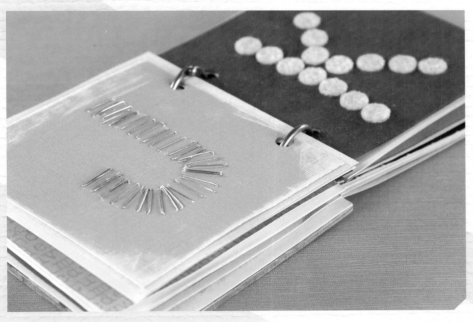

Letterforms Created from Something Else

Summer
by Cathy

Mat several photos with white cardstock. Tear some edges here and there. For the title, stamp each letter with VersaMark ink, then cover each stamped "outline" with a different treatment (machine stitching, ribbon, etc.).

WHIMSICAL
Sybil Green

Modern
Chalet Paris 1960

Historic
Clarendon

Little Boy
Giddyup

Grunge
Graham Regular

cartooN
Variex

Choose your font to depict the "tone" of your scrapbook page. Serious, playful, casual...there are many choices in fonts.

Letterforms Created from Something Else

Life is Beautiful
by Emily

Apply paint to background, then press a clean foam stamp into the paint. Create the title from random objects that look like each letter.

Princess
by Jackie

Cut diamonds from patterned paper and stitch in place. Sew small flowers with a beaded center at the end of a few diamond rows. Reverse print title letters onto wrong side of cardstock. Adhere ribbon to right side of cardstock and cut out letters. Using tweezers, fray ribbon for a tattered look.

Pictures
by Cathy

Cut negative strips to form title letters. Attach with eyelets or staples. Create the negative art in Adobe Illustrator using the *Rounded Rectangle* and *Rectangle* tools. Set the quote on a layer below the negative strip; use the *Move* tool to position text. Set the text for the author on the same layer as the quote, and use the *Rotate* tool to rotate the text 90° counter-clockwise.

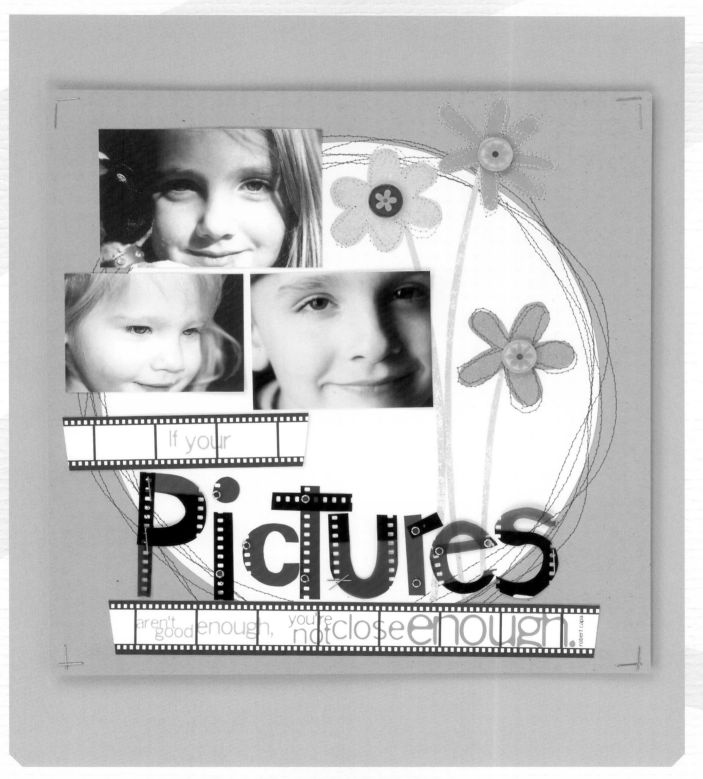

All That I Hope For
by Emily

Print photo onto notebook paper. Frame photo with stamped journaling. Age paper and fill in the circle letter stamps with ink. Stitch paper to background and embellish areas with decorative tape. Stitch stems on the flowers.

Bittersweet
by Ashley

To cut stamps, cut blocks of SoftCut to desired letter size. Hand letter words/letters in reverse. Cut out negative space with carving tools. To make layout, layer papers and fabric on background. Stamp journaling on notebook paper using watercolors. (Paint watercolors onto stamp using a paintbrush.) When dry, outline letters in pen. Stitch main photo to page. Hand cut large scallop-edge border; secure hand-cut circles to the center with pins, brads or buttons.

1. The girls love seeing pages with their favorite puppy.

2. Roxie is a "velcro dog" so she is always around. Therefore, getting her picture is easy.

3. Roxie is my therapy... helps me amazingly with my depression. I am thankful for that.

4. When we get the camera out, Roxie looks right at it and tilts her head to pose.

5. Roxie is part of our family... and therefore our family scrapbooks.

6. She is so stinkin' cute!

I catch myself scrapbooking my dog as often as the girls and family. Some people wonder why. My answers are simple...

ROXIE 2004

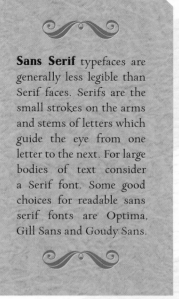

Sans Serif typefaces are generally less legible than Serif faces. Serifs are the small strokes on the arms and stems of letters which guide the eye from one letter to the next. For large bodies of text consider a Serif font. Some good choices for readable sans serif fonts are Optima, Gill Sans and Goudy Sans.

Stamped Type

Roxie
by Jennifer

Stamp on photo and paper. Stamp some of the letters onto orange cardstock. Cut out and adhere in place. Machine stitch circles around journaling.

Stamped Type

Grin
by Nia

Create title in Word, leaving an open space for "grin". Print out. Print the same title block again on printer paper, this time typing the bottom word "grin". Using this second printed sheet as a stencil, cut out the inside of "grin" and "nothing". Place the paper stencil over the title and stamp within the stencil area of the two cut-out words. Let dry and lift to reveal pattern. Place photo and patterned paper on page and embellish with metal tags and buttons.

nothing IN THE WORLD IS AS SWEET AS A LITTLE BOY'S GRIN (NOTHING)

austin

Upside Down
by Jen

Photocopy comics. Place photocopy print-side down on the back side of acrylic letter. Rub a xylene blender pen over the back of the photocopy until the image transfers. Attach notebook paper to the red cardstock. Before adhering the acrylic letters, use a fine-point pen to trace the letters several times, slightly shifting the letter each time. Print journaling on background cardstock and add photos, title and embellishments. Adhere acrylic letters with spray adhesive.

Fridge Magnets
by Jackie

Paint small wooden discs or cover with patterned paper. Add rub-on letters and embellish with small accents such as mini buttons.

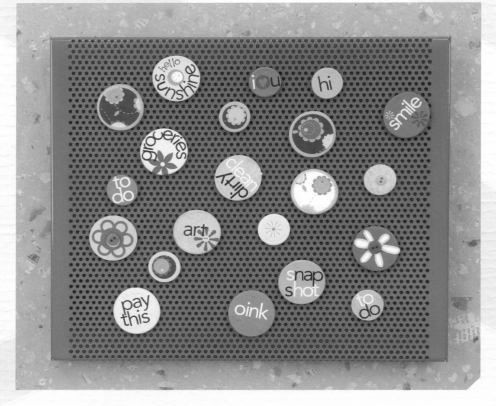

Halloween Apples
by Jackie

Tear the first layer off the upper left corner of corrugated cardboard. Add patterned paper and a cardstock block border. Fill a text box with black and change the text to white. Print on orange cardstock. Use various media for the title letters.

Jump High
by Renee

To create title blocks, cover chipboard pieces with vintage book paper, sand and peel some edges. Iron on title letter following package instructions. Add sanded chipboard letter on top. Layer photos and papers onto background page. Adhere journaling, tab and title pieces using machine stitching.

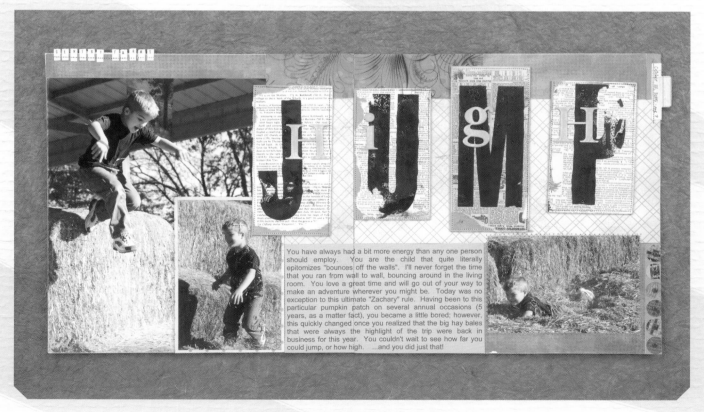

4

CHAPTER FOUR

Make A

statement

When you want to make a fashion statement, you'll probably head for the bright colors, distinctive materials or wild accessories. Just as you can make a statement with clothing, you can also make a statement with typography. Here you'll see how to take letterforms and text and turn them into art. Whether it's making flower petals from graduating colors of text or varying the size of the text to form an interesting block of text, you'll be tempted to try these fashionable ideas. Be brave and put a bold new spin on otherwise common typographic treatments to create pages that will turn heads.

When combining typefaces, be dramatic, particularly with larger elements on the page. Combine unexpected type styles instead of very similar styles. Vary weight, sizing, etc. to highlight the differences.

Little Star
by Renee

For the title, create several text blocks in Photoshop. Manipulate the size, and stretch using text features to create a justified title block in varying font sizes and weights. Print and adhere to background. Add journaling block, photos and a stitched star.

> If you space your kerning too wide, it gets hard to read copy.

Keep your kerning/tracking tight in body copy to make it easily legible. If the letters are spaced too far apart, it is difficult and uncomfortable for the eye to read the text.

When friends forsake you and turn against you, don't despair. Look up and know that there is one in control of every aspect of your life. Everything is in God's hands. He said that He sees the littlest sparrow when it falls. He even knows the number of each hair on your head. Why would you ever wonder what is in store for you or even begin to worry? You are His child and a part of His kingdom. There is never any reason for you to fret or even be concerned of what your tomorrow holds. He has fashioned each star in the heavens which are more numerable than could ever be counted, yet He still is concerned about you. Though He fashioned so many stars, He still chose to fashion you in His image. Even when you're feeling little and non-essential, you are big in His eyes. He's never too busy to be concerned about you. You will always be His little star. –July 2005

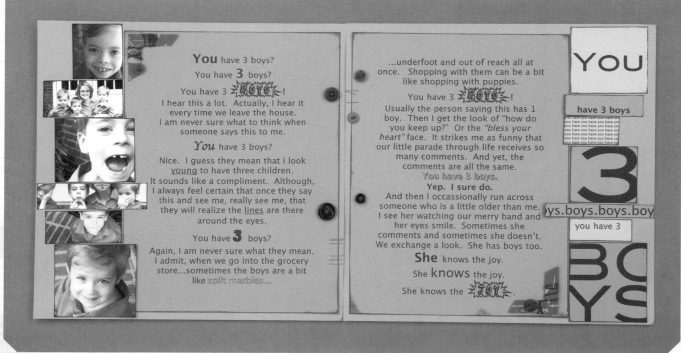

You Have 3 Boys
by Kelli

Make title and page border from several text boxes. Put a word, number or phrase in each one, and alter the size and spacing. Print and cut into squares.

THING about **CANADA'S WONDERLAND** *to a four year old* the (HUGS) and hand shakes from the *FAMOUS* At first you were *SHY* but **you** warmed up to **the idea of** *hangin' with your* "**IDOLS**" *quickly.* Soon you **were** searching them out and **making sure** was there to capture your *"moments"* on film.

BRUSH WITH FAME

Vary Font Size or Weight

Brush with Fame
by Leslie

Type journaling and vary the color and size of the words and lines. Use only one font, but change some to bold and some to italics. Make background from patterned papers cut in various shapes. Add journaling box and title. Print date on small jewelry tags and hang on layout.

Vary Font Size or Weight

Butterfly
by Ashley

Create journaling block in a photo-editing program; use Layers to arrange words until you create an artistic flow within the text. Adjust the size, weight and color of some words. Layer patterned papers on background; stitch journaling block in place. Add fabric, then stitch swirls onto fabric. Embellish page with buttons, tags and charms.

Halloween 2005

she wanted to be a **blue butterfly** with and she knew she needed **movie star glasses** because all butterflies do.

Summer Lily

Combine Upper & Lowercases

Holy Cow, He's Twelve!
by Marilyn

Collage patterned papers for background. Use sandpaper to make a rubbing of chipboard letters that spell *"twelve"*. Continue the rubbing onto one of the photos that was printed on white cardstock. Make additional rubbings of chipboard letters with colored pencils. Frame with slide holders.

Combine Upper & Lowercases

Six Going on Seven
by Lisa

For the title, type each word in its own text box. Make each letter a different font, color, size and horizontal alignment. Use the *Move* tools to overlap words and use the *Arrange* tools to set overlap and placement. Type an additional line of text (*"going on"*) vertically on the page. Type journaling in a new text box. Print, then add photos and a pre-printed transparency to the top.

Combine Upper & Lowercases

Loving Summer
by Jackie

Print title letters in various colors on white cardstock. Trim around each letter, leaving only a thin, white outline on the outside. Adhere to patterned paper and add a few staples for embellishments. Use a circle punch to cut a circle out of ribbon and adhere to a metal-rimmed tag. Use the tag as an *"O"* in the title. Dot the *"I"* with a button.

Combine Upper & Lowercases

Perfect Moment
by Cathy

Using Adobe Illustrator, type text, then convert to paths. Group the letters of each individual word, then give each sentence shape by enlarging and reducing the words. Keep playing with scale and positioning until you reach the desired composition. Cut flower petals and stem from pieces of patterned paper. Randomly hand stitch on layout with a needle and embroidery floss.

In text that is typeset for scrapbooking or any graphic design, it is not acceptable to use two spaces in between your sentences. This is a common mistake since this is what is taught in school when writing papers, etc (where it *is* acceptable to use two spaces).

Coloring of Type

Dear Granny
by Kelli

Kelli wanted to emphasize the fading memory of her grandmother through the fading of the text. Make every few lines of text a lighter color of ink.

Coloring of Type

This Moment
by Jennifer

Create journaling in Word. Change color of letters to make the rainbow effect. Add stitching at the top in different colors to emphasize the font colors.

07.04.03
meghan grendell
beautiful baby girl
cooperative & happy
always smiling
LOVED

Meghan
by Leslie

For journaling, create separate text boxes filled with different colors. Add text in different colors, as well. Cut into a circle and into strips to make the circle text section. Print descriptive words (in pink) inside a green text box and place it behind hand-cut swirl section in upper left corner.

Coloring of Type

Birthday Girl
by Marilyn

Assemble white cardstock, patterned papers and photos on background. Trace letters for "*birthday*" and cut out from white cardstock, revealing background. Poke holes and stitch outlines of letters. Paint insides of letters with a Q-tip. Print journaling onto oatmeal cardstock and cut into a circle.

BIRTHDAY

GIRL

Amelia had two parties and two cakes this year. Goes well with the fact she turned two. We had a small party for her at Grandpa and Grandma Healey's house earlier in the week and they gave her a dancing Care Bear and a neat little kitchen with play food and pots and pans. Her favorite present at her second party was a new bike to ride outside. She immediately started trying to ride it; which was mostly just walking with it between her legs. Mommy took pictures of her that morning, which turned out great!

MNOPQRSTUVW

February 2005

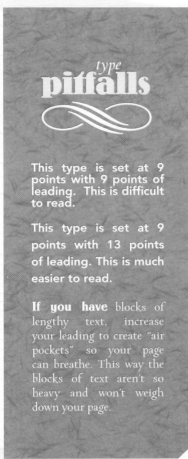

type pitfalls

This type is set at 9 points with 9 points of leading. This is difficult to read.

This type is set at 9 points with 13 points of leading. This is much easier to read.

If you have blocks of lengthy text, increase your leading to create "air pockets" so your page can breathe. This way the blocks of text aren't so heavy and won't weigh down your page.

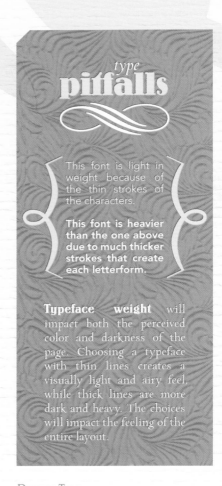

type **pitfalls**

This font is light in weight because of the thin strokes of the characters.

This font is heavier than the one above due to much thicker strokes that create each letterform.

Typeface weight will impact both the perceived color and darkness of the page. Choosing a typeface with thin lines creates a visually light and airy feel, while thick lines are more dark and heavy. The choices will impact the feeling of the entire layout.

Reverse Type

Seaside Ave.
by Danielle

Using photo-editing software, merge three photos into one, convert to grayscale and adjust the contrast for an extreme effect. Make the light areas white so the orange cardstock shows through cleanly when printed.

Reverse Type

Friends
by Tina

Draw a starburst directly on background paper. Cut out each ray of the starburst using an X-Acto knife. Inside a text box, typeset the words and phrases to fit within each starburst. Fill the inside of the text box with the background color and change the text color to white. Print each of the text boxes on a transparency and layer each behind the appropriate ray. Add strips of patterned paper and a small embellishment in the center.

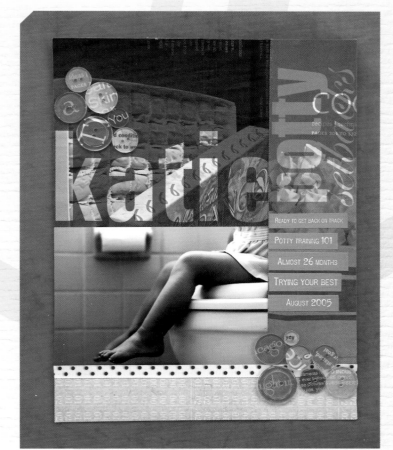

Potty Setbacks
by Nia

Using Photoshop or other editing software, create title blocks, setting the type to white and the background to deep brown. Trim a magazine page (or patterned paper) to size of the created blocks and run through printer. Be sure to choose a paper light in color so the text is readable once printed. Adhere title blocks to page. Back clear buttons with words cut from a magazine. Print journaling, setting type to white and background to pink; trim into strips. Adhere patterned paper, magazine pages or custom printouts containing interesting letters and phrases to the back of clear buttons to create custom embellishments.

Finding His Sport
by Lisa

For title, create six square text boxes with green and orange fill. Use corner tools to round corners. Create six additional text boxes with title text and letters, setting text to white/clear. Arrange over text boxes in a varying pattern. For journaling, create one large text box with orange fill and rounded corners. Type text, setting color to white/clear. Use text tools to adjust indents from either side, justification and leading. For accent strips at the bottom, create two text boxes with green fill and rounded corners. Type dingbats as you would text, setting color to white/clear.

Blue
by Tina

Create circular paths in Photoshop. Set text on the paths, then use the *Character* palette to change the font, size and spacing of the type so it wraps entirely around each path (the goal is to create a perfectly spaced circle of type). Print onto background. Hand cut rings from patterned paper to fit around the outside of the type circles. Crop corners of photos to fit behind rings. Add embellishments inside the ring and hand stitch additional circles as accents.

Traci and Oren
by Jen

Create wave path in Photoshop and type text along the path. Print and cut out. Layer background papers and photos, layering the wave on top of the seam where the background papers meet. Add acrylic letters and embellishments. Hand journal along the wave.

FOR A BRIEF MOMENT IT'S GLORY AND BEAUTY, BELONG TO OUR WORLD...

FLIES ON AND ALTHOUGH WE WISH IT COULD

LIKE SUN BEAM BUT THEN

WE ARE THANKFUL TO HAVE SEEN IT AT ALL

HAVE STAYED

BESIDE US

A BUTTERFLY LIGHTS

MARK ANTHONY WHYTE

WITH US FOR 3 SHORT YEARS

Mark Anthony Whyte by Leslie

Crumple vellum and layer over background. Stitch on photos. Cut journaling into individual letters and adhere in a swirl shape.

FAMILY PROFILE

FAMILY NAME:
PREFERRED NAMES SHOULD BE THE NAME OF THE DOMINANT MEMBER OF YOUR GANG

HOME ADDRESS:

I got to TOUR the Al HAMBRA
By Myself Because Coop got
Sick. ETHAN STAYED
It was so relaxing
this ZEN-LIKE
So SERENE. I
insiDE. So at

Back.
TOURING
PLACE.
FELT SO CALM
PEACE.

*THIS FORM MAY BE USED TO LIST INTERESTING FAMILY MEMBERS WITH IDENTIFYING PHO
*BE SURE TO INCLUDE ALL MEMBERS THAT HAVE A TALENT OR AN ORIGINAL INFIRMITY OR
*LARGE NOSES AND FUNNY BALDING PATTERNS SHOULD BE CAREFULLY NOTED.
*CHILDREN AND FAMILY PETS SHOULD NOT BE GROUPED TO AVOID CUTENESS OVERLOAD.
ALONE. WITH MY thoughts & this BEAUTIFUL Place.

APPROVED BY: January 2005.

ALL FORGERIES SHOULD BE LEGIBLE AND CLEAR.   USE CONVINCING CHANGES IN HANDWRITING.   BE SURE TO WIPE ALL FINGERPRINTS FROM PHOTOS.   IF APREHENDED -PRE AMERICAN.

 Danielle uses a strong initial cap and a variety of wood type inspired fonts to create a striking title.

Granada
by Danielle

Arrange letters for "*Granada*" in Photoshop around a photo. Give all letters– except "*G*" – low opacities to make them subtle. Print the title and photo directly on the patterned paper in the background. Layer several matted photos and add rub-ons for artistic effect.

Sailor
by Rhonna

For title, use *Text* tool and type "*sailor*". On a new layer, drag and drop photo. Press *Ctrl + Alt + G*. This will group previous layers together, so the photo will only "adhere" to the type. You can also use the *Move* tool to move the photo around until you get it to desired location. Add a *Drop Shadow* for depth.

Great Salt Lake
by Marilyn

Form letters from thin strips of blue cardstock. Add a strip of green cardstock along bottoms of photos. Cut wavy strips of blue cardstock; add to bottom of pages. Cover with plain vellum that has been printed with phrases. Stamp large words onto vellum.

Recipe Card
by Carmen

Bind papers in a tri-fold booklet using three punched holes and a blanket stitch. Insert a recipe with a rounded tab at the top. Close booklet with a long strip of paper.

Type as Art

Heart
by Emily

Print photo onto canvas paper. Paint acrylic wash all around the photo. Lightly sketch a heart, and fill in the shape with various alphabet stamps. When dry, erase pencil lines.

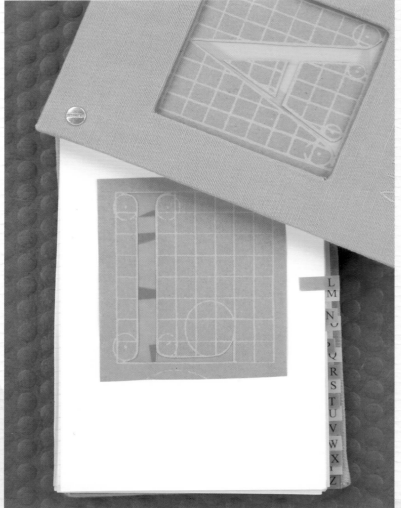

Type as Art

Address Book
by Carmen

Cut out the inside of silk-screened letters (cut from wrapping paper). Back the open letter with vellum. Glue letter tabs on the side of each letter section. Cut a large square in one piece of davy board for cover. Cover davy board with fabric to make a front and back cover. Bind in one corner with a Chicago screw.

Type as Art

Love Blooms »→
by Danielle

Layer the phrase *"love blooms"* on top of each other and gradually space it out towards the top of the petals. Decrease the opacities and spacing at the top, as well. Use the same technique to make the center of the flower. Print and mount on pop dots in a flower shape

Chocolate
Chunk Macaroons

a sweet note

5
CHAPTER FIVE

Incorporating
text

Storytelling and documenting memories is at the heart of scrapbooking. If we are going to tell our story, we must use text. These projects demonstrate a multitude of ways to incorporate text on a project. Notice all the text in Renee's *Excerpts* layout and how it works well with the photos. And see how Cathy records an entire interview on one layout without making the page look burdened with text. Next time you have extensive text to document, don't hesitate to make the text the central focus of the design; it can easily become an extension of the art itself.

Leading is the distance from the baseline of one line of type to another. This can be adjusted depending on the feel you are hoping to achieve.

Tinkerbell
by Leslie

Make background from strips of patterned paper and photos. Type journaling; alter the spacing between the lines to fit script text in between. Collage embellishments under journaling, and add pompom trim along a few vertical seams.

Live in the Moment
by Lisa

For journaling, create one full page text box. Use text tools to alter fonts, colors, sizes and leading. Add pilchrow signs between paragraphs. For title, create a text box and use *Word Wrap* or *Type on a Path* function to add text around the outside of the box. Affix small, embellished tags to the title block.

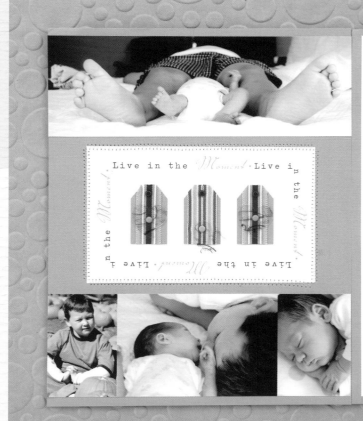

Three
by Jen

Print flower on white cardstock and cut out. Type journaling in a purple text box with white and green text. Add to background along with cut-out flower. Punch flowers and temporarily adhere to back of acrylic piece. Lightly brush white paint over the back of the acrylic. Use rub-ons and epoxy stickers to embellish the front. Print photo on canvas paper and attach to front. Mount layout on foam board to support weight of layout.

You Save Me
by Jennifer

Create journaling in Photoshop. Rotate the journaling box to 45 degrees. Line up in grid pattern and print on white cardstock. Embellish with buttons, flowers, ribbon and machine stitching.

type combos

Combine many weights of text to create texture on your page. Mix very fat or thick fonts with very thin fonts and medium weight fonts. The diversity creates a pleasing texture.

Combine a maximum of 2 or 3 typefaces. Try a serif, a sans serif and a script. A similar feeling (for example, whimsical) will unify your type.

Once you know the rules, go ahead and break a few of them! Look to visionaries like David Carson to see what intelligent disregard of the "rules" can create.

Busy Busy Busy
by Leslie

Create text boxes in various colors; add text in different colors, flipping the orientation of some of the words. Print on 12" long white cardstock to make a border/title for page. Zigzag stitch across each text box to form pockets to hold the journaling.

Barcelona Spain
by Rhonna

Use various brushes and fonts to create page elements. Add freehand drawing around the journaling text with a Wacom Tablet to create the buildings of text. Enlarge photo and apply an *Overlay Light* mode for the background, adjusting the opacity for subtlety. Apply various photo filters to each of the photos.

i AM alWaYS CreATiNG

WheN i AM iNSPiReD

KiD aRT & coloRFUL MesS

i HaVe PRoJeCTS ALL iN PRoCeSS

This ROOM iS LiKe My BRaiN... So MuCh GoiNG oN!

THe bULLeTiN boARD iS ALwAYS FULL...

SoMeTimeS LiKe THis

This is MY CREATiVE SPACE & iT'S iNSPiReD

PiLLoW & FiLL LoVeR

Msc. excerpts from "The Complete Life's Little Instruction Book"

They might be worthwhile someday... you never know what life's going to throw your way, so you had better be prepared.

#847 Pray. There is immeasurable power in it.

#37 Make new friends but cherish the old ones.

#940 Never be ashamed of laughter that's too loud or singing that's too joyful.

#97 Always have something beautiful in sight, even if it's a just a daisy in a jelly glass.

#995 Love someone who doesn't deserve it.

#1167 Be happy with what you have while working for what you want.

#103 Think big thoughts, but relish small pleasures.

#775 Trust in God, but lock your car.

#1024 Follow your own star.

$153 Stand at attention and put your hand over your heart when singing the national anthem.

#1027 Don't get too big for your britches.

#273 Leave everything a little better than you found it.

#1332 Become the world's most thoughtful friend.

#1040 Never go near a kid who's holding a water hose unless you want to get wet.

#883 Never say, "My child would never do that."

#88 Remember that ignorance is expensive.

#1316 Never tell anybody they can't sing.

#1473 Ask yourself if what you're doing today is getting you closer to where you want to be tomorrow.

#374 Take charge of your attitude. Don't let someone else choose it for you.

#186 Become the most positive and enthusiastic person you know.

#119 Put a lot of little marshmallows in your hot chocolate.

#43 Never give up on anybody. Miracles happen every day.

#45 Show respect for teachers.

#826 Act with courtesy and fairness regardless of how others treat you. Don't let them determine your response.

#1083 Remember the three universal healers: calamine lotion, warm oatmeal, and hugs.

#1143 Never let the odds keep you from pursuing what you know in your heart you were meant to do.

#1277 Hold puppies, kittens, and babies any time you get the chance.

#671 Open your arms to change, but don't let go of your values.

#674 Before taking a long trip, fill your tank and empty your bladder.

#676 Mind your own business.

#699 Don't believe all you hear, spend all you have, or sleep all you want.

#1314 Remember that life's most treasured moments often come unannounced.

#444 Laugh a lot. A good sense of humor cures almost all of life's ills.

#335 Reread your favorite book.

#330 Live your life as an exclamation, not an explanation.

#428 Don't accept "good enough" as good enough.

#965 Never ignore evil.

#968 Remember this statement by Coach Lou Holtz: "Life is 10% what happens to me and 90% how I react to it."

#588 Every so often, invite the person in line behind you to go ahead of you.

#594 Remember that no time spent with your children is ever wasted.

#595 Remember that no time is ever wasted that makes two people better friends.

random pictures random thoughts

Orientation

My Creative Space
by Kelli

Adhere photos to background. Use acrylic paint to make a round asterisk-like shape, going over a few photos. Apply a variety of rub-ons, brads and eyelets over the shape.

Columns

Excerpts
by Renee

Type journaling in Word along left side of a 12"x12" formatted page. Leave space for photos and accents. Print onto various shades of cardstock, then cut into strips. Adhere to background, leaving space between each one. Add photos, chipboard embellishments and machine stitching.

Baseball »→
by Jen

Layer file folder, patterned paper, journaling and photos on cardstock. Add rub-ons and embellishments. For the title, layer chipboard letters over letter stickers.

Linework

Ready
by Tina

To incorporate a large amount of text, place each paragraph from right to left in a zigzag pattern. Print onto background paper. Machine stitch overlapping boxes around the text and photos.

Linework

Baby Girl
by Lisa

In a graphics or word-processing program, create individual text boxes for each blurb. Alter font, size, fill color, text color, rotation and placement. For dotted lines, use the line tool to draw, then change stroke to dotted. For circle shapes, use the elliptical shape tool to draw circles and change stroke to dotted. Add patterned circles inside dotted circles and embellish.

[aug.05]

the great american pastime

Check you out with your box of popcorn. You saw your first live

BASEBALL GAME

when I was in Wisconsin. By all reports, you loved it. See the

RALLY HAT?

Your idea. Don't know where it came from, but you did it.

THE BATS

even won the game. And I am sure Uncle Dave had fun

HANGING OUT

with you and Daddy since he is a huge baseball fan.

BASEBALL

 Jen overlapped a mix of fonts for her title, allowing her to fit a long word into a small space. The variety of fonts also adds visual interest to the page.

Interview
with my almost 7 year old

What is your all time favorite book?
"The Diary of a Worm"
then you recited your favorite line
"no matter how many times she looks in the mirror
her face will always look just like her rear end."

What cracks you up?
Brynn

What do you love most about yourself?
I'm a good reader
I have good clothes
I have the prettiest mom in the world)

Favorite all time movie?
Stars Wars III

Color?
black

If you could be animal what would you be?
a mouse because they're fast and intelligent

What are you thinking about right now?
that I wish Cameron (a girl) weren't so hitty - she hurts me

If you could go anywhere in the world where would you go?
that Presidents place - D.C.

What is your favorite part about school?
gym

What scares the bajeebers out of you?
King Cobras

What do you want to be when you grow up?
an Iron Chef (too funny)

What do you like about the world?
that there are 4 seasons -
I wouldn't like it if it were only one all the time

What food could you NOT live without?
Wendy's Chicken Nuggets

What do you wish you could change about yourself?
that I was better at sports

What is your very first memory?
When I kicked the glass in
you purposefully kicked the window (window well window)
that happened to be above my scrap table in . it was
winter - snow, ice and glass everywhere - not a good day!

What would you change about the world?
What don't you like?
that it would never turn dark

What is your favorite Summer memory?
eating pizza at the Salty Dog

Questions, answers and pictures
November 2005

Interview by Cathy
Stamp, paint and stitch on a torn piece of cardboard. Print
questions in one color at a large point size; answers in another
color and smaller. Cut out and adhere around layout.

our trip to the aquarium
was the perfect place to get a
sweet treat after swimming with
the fishes

it was pretty funny
to see you steal daddys cone
for a lick well you pretty
much ate the whole thing

I WAS ABLE TO SNEAK IN A SMALL LITTLE BITE
AS WELL. YUMMERS. AFTER THE QUICK SNACK
WE HEADED TO THE HUGE TANK TO TAKE
A PEEK AT THE BELUGA WHALES.

ice cream

aiden was so excited to get a chance
to see all the fish as was i
the weather was a little cold
but no matter

THERE IS NOTHING QUITE A
SWEET AS
SEEING A LITTLE
CUTIE NIBBLE ON SOME ICE CREAM.

WE ENDED THE DAY BY WATCHING THE TRAINER
FEED THE WALRUS WHICH YOU THOUGHT WAS
ABSOLUTELY HILARIOUS. AS DID I.
A SUPER FUN DAY

The optimum length for lines of text to maximize readability is over 30 characters and under 70 characters. Use columns of text to include a large amount of journaling, like in a newspaper or magazine.

Randomness

Ice Cream
by Nia

Using Photoshop or other word-editing program, type journaling in different sizes and fonts, making sure to change direction of parts of journaling for added effect. Print onto white cardstock. Fill in open spaces with photos and hand-cut shapes.

Randomness

Big Sister Little Sister
by Marilyn

Cut large photo on a curve. Computer generate large words, cut out and use as a stencil. Chalk over stencil onto page. Add photos and embellish with circles, pillows and flowers. Hand write journaling completely over open spaces.

6

CHAPTER SIX

Your handwriting

Why is a famous person's autograph so prized and valuable? Maybe it's because it's a part of who that person is -- something that is unique to him or her and something that can't rightfully be copied or imitated. The same is true with handwriting on a project; it adds a personal touch and provides an opportunity for creative expression. Experiment with your handwriting and try several pen types and surfaces to achieve results that will give your pages a handmade, sentimental and tactile feel.

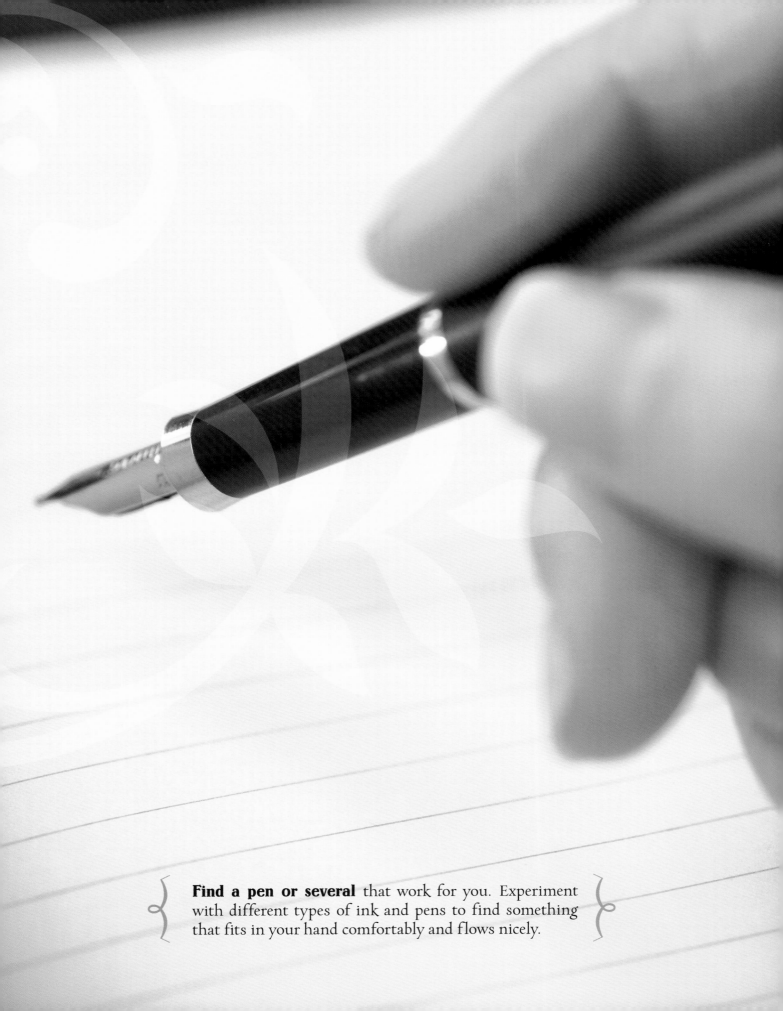

} **Find a pen or several** that work for you. Experiment
with different types of ink and pens to find something
that fits in your hand comfortably and flows nicely. {

Autumn
by Renee

Write descriptive phrases all over 12"x12" cardstock. Turn over and trace leaf pattern onto backside of cardstock. Cut out shape and stitch to patterned paper front. Do the same on orange cardstock but make a smaller leaf. Attach fabric swatches to felt adhesive letters. Trim excess fabric and stitch to page for title. Sew buttons across the bottom.

Anniversary Tips
by Kelli

Cut shape from cardstock. Glue small pieces of inked patterned paper to cover the shape. When dry, trim the excess and ink or use a marker around the edges. Hand write greeting with black pen.

Anniversary gift tip #321

A "Hey Honey, do you want to shake it first?" doesn't add to the excitement of unwrapping an oven mit

[Best not to shop for "Honey" in the kitchen dept.]

Anniversary gift tip#52

A Spatula Wrapped prettily is still a Spatula

[there is no "plastic" Anniversary]

Anniversary gift tip #308

"Never give a gift that can be used against you as a weapon"

[The 6th Anniversary is IRON...but an iron Skillet is not an acceptable gift.]

Self Portrait
by Marilyn

On pink cardstock, write words with a brown brush-tipped marker. Print journaling over handwriting. Adhere to page with photo and floral patterned papers.

All Things Great
by Ashley

Layer ribbon and orange tape under photo. Add a felt flower over the top. Stitch circles of tissue paper to background and embellish with colored brads. Hand letter title and journaling; fill in with watercolor.

handwriting HELPERS

Try writing the alphabet or a single word and fitting it into different spaces -- tall and thin, or shorter and wide. Loosen your hand before you begin. Take a piece of plain paper and doodle, draw flowing lines, circles or anything to loosen your wrist and warm up your hand for writing.

30 days hath September, april, june and november; all the rest have 31, excepting february alone, and it twenty-eight days time, but in leap years, february has twenty nine. ✱2006✱

Jackie's adorable handwriting gives this piece a definite hand-made feel that's hard to achieve on a computer. For even spacing, write lightly in pencil before tracing in pen.

30 Days
by Jackie

Cut decorative tags from several different patterned papers. Attach a small calendar month to each tag and arrange on background. Fasten tags to background with a variety of fasteners. Paint frame and distress with sandpaper. Hand print the poem using a waterproof ink marker.

That Bird
by Rhonna

Cut patterned paper to insert the photo behind. Apply rub-ons to the photo. Hand write on the photo using a Wacom Tablet and add a few flourishes.

My Angel
by Emily

Write letters in pencil, then go over roughly in pen, making lines form a scratchy look.

Stand and Deliver
by Jen

Use photo-editing software to make a green stripe on the photo. Print photo and mount on white cardstock. Paint green and gray stripes around the photo. When dry, hand write on the strips. Paint the word "Stand" on gray cardstock. When dry, print journaling over the top.

Notes to Self
by Tina

Hand write on a variety of labels. Position over background in a collage style with a several embellishments.

At first while taking this **picture** I was just trying to capture the movement and fun you were having.

Then all of a sudden a ton of **memories** rushed through me of when Phebe and I used to do the exact same thing.

It was **beautiful** actually - as weird as that may seem.

Those were some **carefree** and cherished memories I have and I can't even tell you how happy it makes me to see you making some of your own. ☺

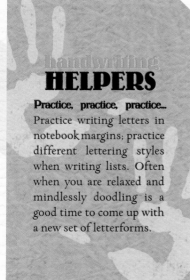

handwriting HELPERS

Practice, practice, practice... Practice writing letters in notebook margins; practice different lettering styles when writing lists. Often when you are relaxed and mindlessly doodling is a good time to come up with a new set of letterforms.

Incorporating Your Handwriting

Carefree Memories
by Cathy

Hand write journaling onto strips; adhere to layout. Computer generate key words and print out. Stitch to layout over side of enlarged photo. Coat buttons with glue, then cover with glitter.

Incorporating Your Handwriting

Very Soon
by Jennifer

Tear strips of fabric and adhere to layout along with photos. Use black pen to write on the fabric.

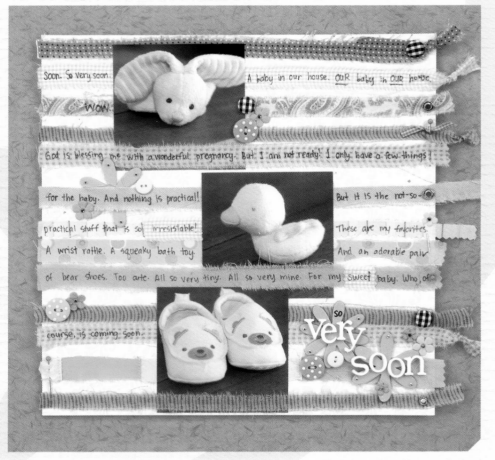

Soon. So very soon. A baby in our house. OUR baby in OUR house. WOW.

God is blessing me with a wonderful pregnancy. But I am not ready! I only have a few things for the baby. And nothing is practical! But it is the not-so-practical stuff that is so irresistable! These are my favorites. A wrist rattle. A squeaky bath toy. And an adorable pair of bear shoes. Too cute. All so very tiny. All so very mine. For my sweet baby. Who, of course, is coming soon.

very soon

Love is All You Need
by Tina

Write words in cursive on blank paper. Cut out to use as a template. Pin pattern to felt and cut out. Add hand stitching to one word. Adhere to layout.

She's Three
by Ashley

Machine stitch blocks of paper to cardstock. Add photos and stitch around the outside. Stamp frames onto light-colored textured cardstock. Hand letter title, one letter to each stamped block, and fill in with watercolors.

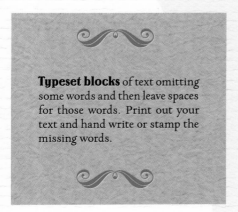

I Love You
by Rhonna

With a Wacom Tablet and a round brush, draw the "I ♥ U" icon and save as a .png file. Drag and drop the icon onto the layout. Journal in a different color. Open focus photo and adjust the opacity levels. Create the polka-dot border by varying the size and color of the round brush, adjusting the spacing and creating a decorative border. Cut out smaller photos in circles, and on a New Layer above the photos, use a lined circle brush to frame the photos.

Typeset blocks of text omitting some words and then leave spaces for those words. Print out your text and hand write or stamp the missing words.

Kay
by Jennifer

Print large letters on scrap paper. Cut out and trace onto large tags with pencil. Use black and pink pens to fill letter with words. Erase pencil and embellish.

I LOVE YOUR SMILE & your LAUGHTER in this photo. I love how happy we look together. We go thru these GROWING PAINS together. Being a little boy...being a mom. You're figuring THINGS OUT & SO AM I. BUT always together. YOU & ME.

IOWA • MAY • 2005

and me...Where else would I want to be

MARK AND ELLYN'S WEDDING

You & Me
by Danielle

Print photo onto blue cardstock. Draw title letters on cardstock with a black fine-tip pen and embellish with a white paint pen and colored markers. Cut out and adhere to page. Draw random lines in the background and hand write journaling.

You+Me
by Carmen

Create text on computer and print on photo paper. Cut coupons into strips and bind with waxed linen. Write on pages with a silver felt-tip marker.

Once a month, at least...

I would like to spend more quality time with you!

Ideas for the year

we meet there...and dressed up!

you + me
you + me
you + me

other massages
important...for the sou
you +

you + me
you + me

Make Some Tea
by Kelli

Kelli used 11 different writing instruments in the journaling. Use each one two or three times for continuity and use arrows and curves to help guide the eye. Wear protective eyewear and gloves before cutting the license plate. Draw flowers on the back of the plate with a marker and cut out with heavy-duty scissors.

Pen Selection

Because Card Set
by Jackie

Fasten separate card front and back together with a folded circle and a staple. Add red heart cutouts and bits of ribbon; finish with handwritten greeting in two different ink colors.

Handwriting on Surfaces

Willow Beach
by Ashley

Layer papers and photos over a 12"x12" printed transparency. Layer patterned paper under transparency and secure. Cut short lengths of paper tape and trim with scallop-edge scissors; use for title and journaling. Make a flower from red tape and rick rack. Use a photo turn and flower brad to create the center.

Handwriting on Surfaces

Chloe Observations
by Leslie

Journal on a red transparency with a marker designed for slick or glossy surfaces. Use chipboard letters for the title.

handwriting HELPERS

If the spacing of your writing is off a little, add a swirl, a star or a little doodle to make it look like you planned it that way.

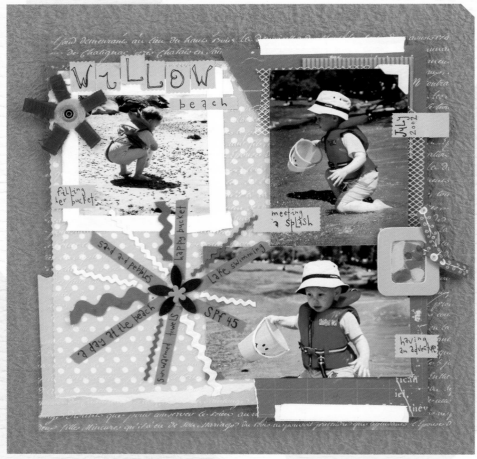

Feel free to play, mixing handwriting and computer fonts. Notice the contrast between the clean, modern sans serif computer font background and Jennifer's printing and doodles.

Wood Greetings
by Jennifer

Write on wood circles with black pen. Use red marker to highlight around the edge. Use circles for a flower center on a card, as a tag on a box or as an "o" in a word.

The Boy Can Eat
by Marilyn

To make circles for background, stamp and emboss, then cut rings with a Coluzzle nested template. Print strip of photos and adhere at an angle. Paint white fun foam with acrylic paint. Adhere two circles of painted foam to page and journal with a pen.

Doodle Cake
by Kelli

For each layer of the cake, repeat a figure-eight shape using a white marker. Outline with a black fine-tip pen. For the title, write each letter on a rectangle and adhere to background.

Yum!
by Danielle

Adjust the Levels of a photo to make a subtle background. (Danielle used a photo of the side of an ice-cream truck.) Desaturate the photo to make the color more faded and soft. Mat photo with teal cardstock and scallop the edge. Layer strips of patterned paper on the right and bottom of the layout. Hand draw doodles directly on the photo and on the strips of patterned paper. Chalk the inside of the "Yum!".

Doodles

Everyday
by Rhonna

Use digital brushes to create the page elements, such as the butterflies used here. Print onto a transparency. Doodle on squares and rectangles, and adhere them to wrinkled tissue paper and cardstock. Finish layout with wisps of paint and die-cut flowers.

Doodles

Welcome to the World
by Cathy

For the boy card, lightly sketch stars on watercolor paper. Stitch several times over the top. For the girl card, stitch circles over and over on watercolor paper. Embellish each card with ribbon and a safety pin.

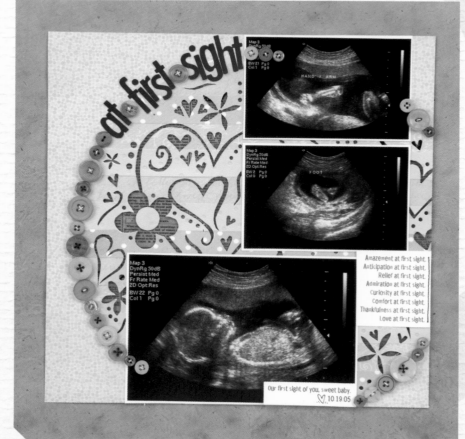

Doodles

Home
by Emily

Dry brush acrylic paint onto watercolor paper. Draw doodles with a pencil and go over a few times in pen. Paint the inside of the doodles with watered-down acrylics.

Doodles

At First Sight
by Jennifer

Cover a cardstock circle with paper strips. Adhere to background. Draw doodles with pencil and cut out. Back layout with a printed transparency.

Doodles

Iris »→
by Ashley

Lay photos on white cardstock. Lightly sketch patterns, border and title around photos. Draw over pencil using pen and nib and permanent ink. Fill in color with watercolor paints. Add ribbon, button and painted tag.

yellow Iris

one of my favourite
spring flowers... a thoughtful
gift from Paul.

spring

 If you're worried that your lettering skills aren't as adept as
Leslie's, loosely trace a printed font. Use transfer paper or a light
table to copy the tracing onto your layout.

Beautiful

by Danielle

Hand write descriptive words that go with the photo using black marker and white paper. Scan into the computer. Arrange photos in Photoshop, then layer scanned words on top of the photo collage. Print collage, then cut out and mount two of the images on foam tape. Hand draw accents around photos and add beads and sequins. Draw photo corners and journal inside.

Path

by Ashley

To create digitally patterned letters, hand write title in ink (1/2" tall). Scan at high resolution and adjust final scan size to 2 ½". Digitally remove color from scanned letters. Select brush, then color and pattern each letter. Print and cut out.

Digital Manipulation of Handwriting

Goals

by Rhonna

Using a Wacom Tablet and a calligraphy brush tip, draw title, frame and numbers. Turn them into brushes and "stamp" in separate layers in different colors. Write journaling under title.

Digital Manipulation of Handwriting

Camera Shy?

by Jen

Cut windows in a square of foam board; cover with paper and place photos behind windows. Attach journaling printed on white cardstock. Use a digital tablet to handwrite "*giggle*" on a 12"x12" canvas; add dingbats for interest. Print onto a transparency. Position the transparency over the layout and attach with ribbon. Adhere chipboard letters for the title.

7

CHAPTER SEVEN

gallery

Jean-Jacques Rousseau noticed, "The world of reality has its limits; the world of imagination is boundless." Our artists prove they are living in the world of imagination as they take the craft of typography to a new realm. In this gallery, they put everything they know into practice to construct pages that delight and inspire. Take note of all the techniques the artists use and how they use type to enhance a theme, convey a message or highlight a photo. The world of typography truly is boundless, so use your imagination and utilize type to add charisma and charm to your works of art.

Display typefaces which include script, distressed, novelty and decorative are best used in smaller doses, particularly for titles, subtitles and other word applications, as opposed to a body of text.

My
friends
have made
THE STORY
OF my LIFE

boy n: a noise with dirt on it.
- not your average dictionary

Oh the places you'll go.
- Dr. Seuss

look

friends
GIVE FULL
COLOR
to OUR lives.

too too

I am just too much.
- Bette Davis

{ **Using typeset words** cut from magazines adds flair to your titles.
Choosing a font with a meandering baseline (or altering the baseline
of individual letters) is another charming option. }

Fabric Swatch Cards & Sweet Sassy Spunky Accents
by Cathy and Jackie

For "Fabric Swatch" cards: Snip little bits of fabric to create letters. Once letters are formed, repeatedly stitch the actual letter over the fabric. Embellish with snippets of ribbon and buttons. *For "Sweet Sassy Spunky" Accents:* Cut pieces of green cardstock and fold one end to form a small flap. Decorate body of accent with ribbon strips and small cardstock circles that are first stamped with a tiny alphabet stamp for the background and then on top with the letter stamp. Tie jute under each flap and fasten with a staple. Cover staple with wire flower accent.

Friends Cards & Journaling Accents
by Cathy and Jackie

For "Friends" cards: Cut words from magazine to make quotation. Adhere to card front. *For "Journaling" Accents:* Fill a small paper bag with a white journaling block decorated with a ribbon tab. For the outer pocket decoration, back preprinted transparency tags with patterned papers; staple on a small quote.

Boy @ 4
by Tina

To create the graffiti on the photos, use black pens and a black crayon to scrawl descriptive words and phrases on white paper. Scan, then open the image in Photoshop and create a brush. Apply the brush directly on the photograph. Erase parts to reveal more of the photo. Selectively color some of the words. Use the same technique to add stars to the other photo. Write title on notebook paper, scan it in and overlay the image directly on the photograph with a slightly reduced opacity.

Run
by Rhonna

Create a custom title and journaling using various fonts. Apply a drop shadow and inner shadow layer style to the title.

Zoom
by Leslie

Type word *"ZOOM"* and then duplicate and overlap the word three more times. Select a different color for each word and adjust their placement so they are off-kilter to give them a sense of movement or blur.

To See the World
by Renee

Overexpose picture of globe and trim to 8.5"x11". Add journaling over the front in layered text boxes. Print additional journaling and cut out each letter. Adhere over printed globe page. Create columns of text for right page, adding printed titles and accents.

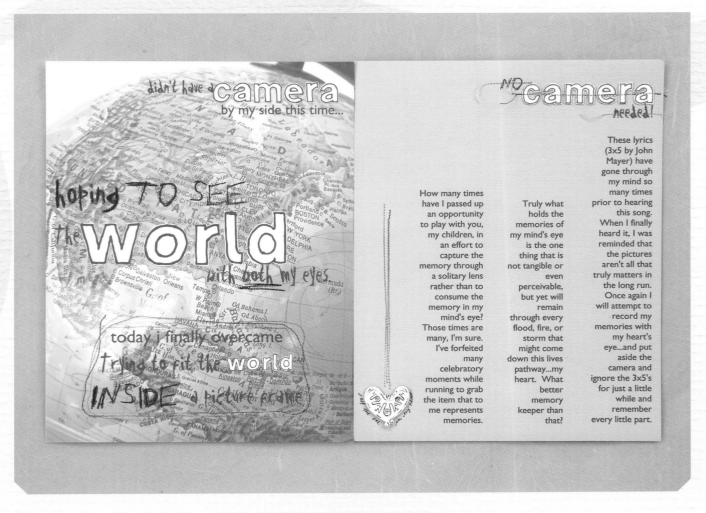

didn't have a **camera** by my side this time...

NO **camera** needed!

hoping TO SEE the **world** with both my eyes

today i finally overcame trying to fit the **world** INSIDE picture frame

How many times have I passed up an opportunity to play with you, my children, in an effort to capture the memory through a solitary lens rather than to consume the memory in my mind's eye? Those times are many, I'm sure. I've forfeited many celebratory moments while running to grab the item that to me represents memories.

Truly what holds the memories of my mind's eye is the one thing that is not tangible or even perceivable, but yet will remain through every flood, fire, or storm that might come down this lives pathway...my heart. What better memory keeper than that?

These lyrics (3x5 by John Mayer) have gone through my mind so many times prior to hearing this song. When I finally heard it, I was reminded that the pictures aren't all that truly matters in the long run. Once again I will attempt to record my memories with my heart's eye...and put aside the camera and ignore the 3x5's for just a little while and remember every little part.

SUMMER VACATION ISN'T THIS WHAT IT'S ALL ABOUT?

summer

this is what it's all About

leisure rules

SUMMER 2005

BOBBY AND AUSTIN

LEISURE RULES

{ } **Marilyn combines** overlapping letters as a mask for part of her subtitle, creating a bold, edgy look.

The Pirate Cowboy Dave
by Kelli

To create the stitched letters "O" and "E," apply a sticker to the fabric and hand stitch over the top.

Flower Notes
by Jackie

Using coordinating solid and patterned paper, cut out hand-drawn or hand-printed loopy flowers and large words. Arrange on cardstock or cork-paper cards.

Leisure Rules
by Marilyn

Make the title by doing several layers. First, cut large, chunky letters in two different shades of light blue to spell "summer." Adhere to the page, overlapping the letters. Next, stamp the sentence in dark brown. Third, add a strip of dark brown cardstock to the bottom of the page. Spell "leisure rules" with two styles of letter stickers. Make sure they are applied well so no paint seeps under them. Dab and spatter green paint over the stickers, completely covering all letters. Remove stickers slowly before paint dries. After paint has dried, apply rub-on letters along the bottom of the page.

It is OK to have white space (empty space on your page that is not filled with text or graphics). It draws attention to your type.

Sewing Letters

Seven
by Cathy

Affix photos to background. Machine stitch a letter on each one to spell out the title.

Journaling Inside a Path

Oil Pastel
by Jen

Print photo and save as version one. In photo-editing software, use the crop tool to create a small photo of a focal area. Crop and re-size the canvas (in white) to about ½" larger than it was. Type journaling around the picture in the white area. Print and save, making sure to rename the photo something different than the master version. Repeat for each focal area. Attach foam to the focal photos and adhere to the large photo. Paint acrylic and chipboard letters for the title.

Take photographs of letters or typeset words to create a unique title for your page.

BEAUTY

The recipe for BEAUTY is to have
less illusion and more Soul,
to retreat from the belief of pain or pleasure
in the body into the
UNCHANGING calm &
glorious freedom of
SPIRITUAL HARMONY.

Sometimes we do before we think. As part of our ongoing effort to involve Aidan in activities that will help him both mentally and physically, we signed him up for Tiger Scouts the first level of Boy Scouts. if you didn't know! What better, more wholesome activity, right? HA!

First off, there's the money. After you buy the Tiger Scout shirt, shorts, belt, socks, hat, kerchief, kerchief band, badges, handbook, etc. you're out well over 150 bucks.

Then there are the meetings. Put 10 6 year old boys in a room with Dads in charge (who clearly don't know how to handle 10 6 year old boys) and they turn into animals. Animals! When Vic was out of town last week, I had to take Aidan in his absence (and coordinate a scrapbooking project, but that nightmare is another layout in the making). I was appalled by how the boys acted. Talking over the leader and hitting each other, yelling, you name it. I was so mad at Aidan that I didn't speak to him for the entire ride home. Sigh...so much for good intentions. My hope is that this does turn into a worthwhile activity eventually. Time will tell.

Anyway, I'm not really sure what the point of all this is other than to emphasize that we should maybe think before enrolling Aidan in future activities. He sure looks cute in his uniform, though, doesn't he?

SEARCH · DISCOVER · SHARE

Tiger Scout

(or, good grief, what have we done?)

Justified text has even edges on both the left and right margins.

Justified text increases readability, unless the line length is short, creating gaps between words.

Flush left text is straight along the left side with an uneven (or ragged edge) on the right.

If setting copy flush left, be aware of very long or short lines.

Flush right is the opposite of flush left.

Flush right can be difficult to read, but it can be effective in small blocks, creating a margin against an edge.

Using Clipping Masks

Beauty
by Rhonna

Make background with various flower brushes; vary the color and opacity. Rotate journaling on its side to give the motion of falling down. To create title, type the text, then put the photo on top of it and create a Clipping Mask, thus filling the font with the photo.

Distressing Type

Tiger Scout
by Lisa

For the title, use the grunge technique adapted from *Photoshop User Magazine*, April/May 2005.

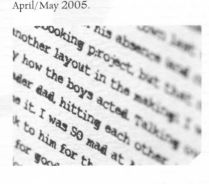

Print Text on Photos

Captivate
by Leslie

Print journaling on white cardstock with colored text boxes and text. Frame under negative transparency frames. Cut patterned paper strips and circles and arrange on page. Add embellishments and photos. Type text on main photo in Photoshop. For each line of text, alter color and opacity to get a faded, dreamy look.

Doodles

Still
by Marilyn

Use a white colored pencil to write text and draw snowflakes onto the dark blue background. Color in some areas with a turquoise pencil. Add small, clear rhinestones to the drawings. Tear a circle in the paper and photo, and adhere letter beads to the negative space.

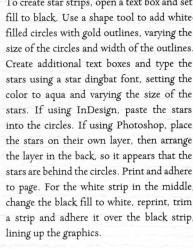

Dingbats Within Circles

Christmas Goober
by Lisa

To create star strips, open a text box and set fill to black. Use a shape tool to add white-filled circles with gold outlines, varying the size of the circles and width of the outlines. Create additional text boxes and type the stars using a star dingbat font, setting the color to aqua and varying the size of the stars. If using InDesign, paste the stars into the circles. If using Photoshop, place the stars on their own layer, then arrange the layer in the back, so it appears that the stars are behind the circles. Print and adhere to page. For the white strip in the middle, change the black fill to white, reprint, trim a strip and adhere it over the black strip, lining up the graphics.

Handwriting on Photo

Photograph
by Emily

Write journaling directly on photo with a marker. Apply rub-ons for the title.

The Many Expressions of Cooper
by Danielle

Decorate a tin to a hold a mini book. Hand draw title with fine-tip colored markers.

Journal on Tags

Brave Girl
by Jennifer

Hand write your journaling on several small jewelry tags (you may want to type your journaling first to use as a reference). Line up tags on layout and secure with decorative brads, adding small silk flowers, ribbon and bits of embroidery thread to each.

{ **LTVWY** }
(unkerned)

{ **LTVWY** }
(correctly kerned)

Letters that frequently require kerning include L, T, V, W or Y, due to either diagonal edges of varying widths from top to bottom. Manual kerning of each letter may be necessary to balance the look of words.

Extra Large Type

Extra Large Type

9 Things
by Leslie

Create background with three different patterned papers. Print a large number on the back of textured green cardstock. Cut out and adhere to layout. Cut strips from background and place journaling behind the holes.

Extra Large Type

Ava Frame
by Lisa

Remove glass and mats from frame. Cut paper into strips and adhere to outer mat. Turn over and use a craft knife to cut out openings. Fill openings of inner mat with patterned paper instead of a photo. Reassemble mats and embellish.

For the letters, type each letter in a graphics or word-processing program. Set the letter to a clear or white fill with a black outline. Reverse print onto the back of several patterned papers. Cut out letters and adhere with pop-dots.

What do you see? 2 boys
Two Men
1 father (and) A Son.
of one mind,
of one soul.
OF ONE heart
when they are together
its a magical thing.
i sit and watch...
have you...

fatherhood

Rhonna uses a Wacom tablet (a pen and tablet device that plugs into your computer) to add handwriting to a digital layout.

Fatherhood
by Rhonna

Create a custom background with various flower brushes; vary the color and opacity. Write journaling on a Wacom Tablet, taking advantage of the pressure sensitivity to look like a brush. Apply a *Wave Warp* to the title.

Mrs. Shields
by Cathy

Affix flower stickers to background. Twist pipe cleaners into circles to frame stickers. Machine and hand stitch them to background. Embellish page with rhinestones and other sparkly embellishments.

Happy Birthday Ellie
by Cathy

Create masking tape labels by running printing paper through printer first. Cover words with masking tape, then run through printer again. Emboss words to seal.

Tea
by Ashley

Place photos on white cardstock. In pencil, sketch patterns, border and title around photo. Draw over pencil using pen and nib and permanent ink. Fill in color with watercolor paints. Sew wood buttons in place.

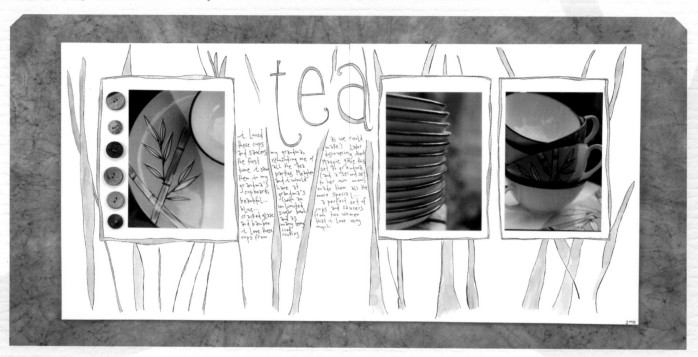

Text Around Photos

Creature Comforts
by Lisa

In Adobe InDesign, use shape tool to create 4 ½"x 5 ½" boxes. Use *Type on a Path* tool to add text for each element, wrapping text around the box. For title, type word in a single font, then use text tools to modify each letter, modifying outline vs. no outline, thin stroke vs. thick, etc. Print and cut out.

We went to 🏠 for the 2peas crop in August 2005. We drove 6 hours in the car one way, just the 2 of us. Of course, that included a stop at ◎. Can't pass by ◎!

The crop was amazing. The women who attended were psyched about cropping. And the other 🪣 GOLDEN GIRLS were as incredible in real life as they are online. Warm, funny, friendly women with a common bond.

👶, you were phenomenally good. You rode in the 🎒 for the 12 hours of the crop and didn't make a 💧. You were totally in your element, smiling & flirting with all the croppers.

charming the scrapbookers in

mr. **flirt**

Rebus Journaling

Mr. Flirt
by Jen

Find images to represent words in the journaling. Type the journaling, leaving spaces for the images. Open each image as a new layer and position in the open space. Print journaling, then layer on page along with photos and patterned paper.

Type Good Enough to Eat

Alphabet Cookies
by Tina

Print monogram letters onto cardstock using a variety of fonts sized between 3-6 inches. Cut out letters to create a template. Roll out sugar cookie or gingerbread dough to ¼" thick. Place the letter on top and cut out each letter using a razor blade or very sharp knife. Bake according to recipe, cool, then decorate with Royal icing.

First Born by Rhonna

Use the *Custom Shape* tool to create the shape of the butterfly. Select the *Type* tool and hover it close to the *Path* line. The cursor will change. Type inside selected shape.

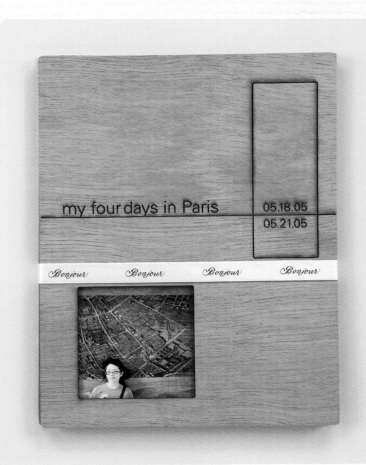

Laser Etch Type

Paris

by Carmen

Glue one end of accordion-folded wrapping paper to front cover and glue the other end to the back cover. Assemble a collage of photos, notes and collectibles to background. Keep book closed with ribbon. Have text laser cut into the wood cover.

Type for Gift Giving

Gift Wrap

by Jennifer

Create circle text using WordArt. Make various sizes of circles with various fonts. Overlap circles and print on cardstock. Wrap gifts and make matching tag.

True Friends
by Nia

In Photoshop, create three 3"x12" text boxes, each with a different background color. Type random, layered text in white, brown and a shade slightly lighter or darker than the color of the text box. Print out strips and cut into 2" squares. Place photo on page, and layer squares randomly around photo, placing some on pop-dots. Print smaller photo and trim to a 2" square, adhering among other squares.

Emboss Handwriting

This Boy
by Emily

Create frame on page with insulation tape. Write into the tape with a stylus or pencil. Paint over the entire frame with black paint, making sure it gets into the grooves. While still wet, wipe off with a paper towel. Paint another color over the top (here, blue) and lightly wipe, leaving some showing.

Add Texture to a Title

Fish
by Leslie

Find a font that resembles fish scales. Print the letters on various colors of cardstock; cut out. Drop dots of Diamond Glaze on the dots of the printed font to give the illusion of wet fish skin.

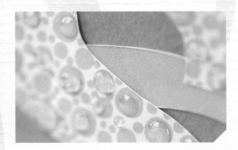

credits

AL: Autumn Leaves   DCWV: Die Cuts With a View   MM: Making Memories   HS: Heidi Swapp   AC: American Crafts   PS: Adobe Photoshop

CI: Creative Imaginations   MAMBI: me and my BIG ideas   BG: Basic Grey   SW: Scrapworks   CB: Chatterbox

Credits: Products without a credit are either part of the artist's personal stash or not available for purchase.
Note: Unless otherwise noted, all computer fonts are downloaded from the Internet. 2Peas fonts are from www.twopeasinabucket.com; CK fonts are from Creating Keepsakes.